LET'S GO TEAM:
Cheer, Dance, March

LET'S GO TEAM:
Cheer, Dance, March

History of
CHEERLEADING

Doris Valliant

Mason Crest Publishers
Philadelphia

Mason Crest Publishers, Inc.
370 Reed Road
Broomall, PA 19008
(866) MCP-BOOK (toll free)
www.masoncrest.com

First printing

1 2 3 4 5 6 7 8 9 10

Library of Congress Cataloging-in-Publication Data

Valliant, Doris.
  History of cheerleading / Doris Valliant.
      v. cm. — (Let's go team—cheer, dance, march)
Includes index.
Contents: What is cheerleading? — The early years — Competitions —
All-star cheerleading — Cheerleading today.
  ISBN 1-59084-534-X
1. Cheerleading—History—Juvenile literature. [1. Cheerleading—History.]
I. Title. II. Series.
  LB3635 .V35 2003
  791.6'4—dc21
                                    2002015990

Produced by
Choptank Syndicate and Chestnut Productions
226 South Washington Street
Easton, Maryland 21601

Project Editors Norman Macht and Mary Hull
Design Lisa Hochstein
Picture Research Mary Hull

Printed and bound in the Hashemite Kingdom of Jordan

OPPOSITE TITLE PAGE

Over the years cheerleading has moved from the sidelines to the center stage. Today's cheerleaders use athletic, gymnastic, and dance skills to wow audiences.

Table of Contents

What Is Cheerleading?

They cheer at Musketeers football games. For each football player, they decorate paper bags and write encouraging slogans, then fill them with candy. They create spirit signs and banners. Like most teenage girls, they complete homework and worry about their appearance.

However, these teenagers are also outstanding athletes and expert gymnasts who do standing back tucks, back handsprings, and heel stretches. They turn their bodies into a series of dizzying tumbles and mount highly difficult partner and pyramid stunts. Some toss their lightest and most agile cheerleaders high in the air. They are the varsity cheerleaders of Kentucky's Greenup County High

The University of Kentucky Wildcats have won more UCA National College Championships than any other college.

School, nine times Universal Cheerleaders Association (UCA) National Champions. The Greenup County High School varsity cheerleaders represent cheerleading today, and they carry on a tradition of leading cheers to boost the crowd's spirits.

Cheerleading began over 100 years ago as simple cheers shouted by yell captains from the sidelines during college football games. Cheerleaders still lead cheers and chants that support a variety of sports teams, but they may be better athletes than the players on the field. Today it takes more than a megaphone and a pretty smile. Candidates trying out for places on the cheerleading squad, whether it's junior high, high school, or college level, need a combination of athletic, gymnastic, and dance skills. Tumbling, pyramids, basket tosses, and any number of complicated gymnastic flips and twists have become the cheerleader's standard repertoire.

School cheerleaders still focus on supporting their athletic teams, especially for football and basketball. However, many of these squads fiercely compete against each other in regional and national competitions held by associations such as the Universal Cheerleaders Association (UCA), National Cheerleaders Association (NCA), and the World Cheerleading Association (WCA). Cheerleaders attend summer camps to learn skills to support school spirit. They also attend to learn the latest stunts and routines that will get them a national championship.

Coaches go to summer camps for the same reasons. Candy Berry, the Greenup County High cheerleading coach, continually looks for new chants, stunts, dances,

Kentucky's Greenup County High School cheerleaders are among the most famous in the nation, known for their innovative and award-winning routines.

and gymnastic twists and flips to teach her squad. Then she trains her squad to perform these complex routines with skill and precision.

The Greenup County varsity cheerleaders have been taking home the UCA national trophy off and on since their first win in 1981. Berry's championship Greenup squad set the standards for Kentucky cheerleading programs all the way through college levels. Nationwide, cheerleading coaches regard Berry as the competitive cheerleading expert.

Berry believes that a championship program supports its cheerleaders in and out of the classroom. That's one of the reasons for Greenup's success. Several other

Kentucky high schools, such as Henry Clay High School in Lexington, boast championship squads, but none can match Greenup County's record.

On the college level, the University of Kentucky has beaten the Greenup record. As of 2002, the University of Kentucky cheerleaders had won 12 UCA National College Championships. Morehead State University ran a close second with 11 championships. At the National Cheerleaders Association (NCA) Collegiate Championships, University of Louisville cheerleaders have taken home eight national titles.

The Greenup County High School cheerleaders and their university counterparts show how far cheerleading has come since college guys with megaphones and popular girls in sweaters and pleated skirts led cheers in front of football fans.

TO CHEER OR TO CHANT?

A cheer is a long routine performed during a time out, between quarters at football and basketball games, or between matches at a wrestling meet. The ball is not in play, so there is time to complete a stunt such as forming a pyramid or doing some tumbling. Cheers can be as elaborate as the skills of a squad can achieve.

A chant is a short phrase of words that is often repeated three or more times. Cheerleaders yell chants from the sidelines, so another name for chants is sidelines. Cheerleaders use chants throughout the game to encourage the players or react to something that happens on the field or court.

Because co-ed squads have greater stunting power, male cheerleaders are in demand.

People skills, however, remain a priority. After all, the purpose of cheerleading has always been to generate enthusiasm to get the crowd involved. Candy Berry believes that what makes a winning squad is the cheerleader's bond with the crowd. Berry points out that the tumbling, dancing, basket tosses, partner stunts, and pyramid and mount sequences all keep the crowd involved, whether it's at the Friday night football game or at a national cheerleading competition.

Getting the crowd enthused is important in professional sports as well. In the 1950s, the Baltimore Colts were the first football team in the NFL to hire a professional cheerleading squad. In the 1960s more pro football and basketball teams incorporated cheerleading squads.

The Baltimore Colts cheerleaders, founded in 1954, were the first cheerleading squad in the National Football League.

Today's professional cheerleaders usually don't lead the crowds in cheers; instead, they are crowd-pleasers themselves. These pro cheerleaders are more like dancers in a chorus line since they are picked for their good looks and dancing abilities, especially the talent to kick high. Professional cheerleaders support teams in the National Football League (NFL) and the National Basketball Association (NBA).

In Canada, the Canadian Football League (CFL) has followed the American showgirl style for their professional cheerleaders, except the Edmonton, Alberta Eskimos, coached by Dianne Greenough. Greenough's Eskimos are unique in the CFL because they are real cheerleaders performing collegiate style co-ed routines with pyramids, tumbling, and partner stunting.

Is cheerleading a sport? High schools and colleges nationwide argue the pros and cons. Fourteen states recognize cheerleading as a sport, and many are considering doing so. In Canada, a few provinces consider cheerleading a sport and treat it as such with all the rules and regulations that govern an athletic team.

Whether it's a sport or a student activity, cheerleading is attracting a growing number of male athletes. They find stunting, tumbling, jumping, and throwing girls high into the air as challenging as playing on the sports field.

"Nothing else like it," says Justin Carrier, a former cheerleader. "Basically, the guy is the frame. The girl's a piece of art." Co-ed squads with their male cheerleaders have enabled the girls to reach higher levels of difficulty in their stunts and routines.

Cheerleading attracts more than three million elementary, high school, and college men and women in the United States, and a growing number in Canada, Great Britain, and Japan. Eighty-three percent of these cheerleaders carry a B average or above in high school. Many of these talented young people also play another sport. Cheerleading has evolved from an all-male activity, to mostly female, to today's highly talented co-ed and all-girl squads. Cheerleaders who can turn flips, dance, tumble, and fly high into the air are some of the most well-rounded athletes on the field today.

The Early Years

The first known cheer heard from the sidelines happened during a Princeton University football game in the late 1880s: "Rah, rah, rah! Tiger, tiger, tiger! Sis, sis, sis! Boom, boom, boom! Ah! Princeton! Princeton! Princeton!" This yell is Princeton's longest used and most distinctive cheer. It is called a "locomotive" cheer because it sounds like a train engine that starts slowly then picks up speed (Tiger, tiger, tiger! Sis, sis, sis! Boom! Boom! Boom!)

Princeton University also established the first pep club. All-male "yell leaders" supported the Princeton football team with cheers from the sidelines.

Cheerleaders began using paper pom pons in the 1930s to accentuate their arm movements, but the vinyl pom pons of today were not invented until the 1960s.

When the yell leaders called for a "tiger," they did not refer to the Princeton University Tiger mascot, because it didn't exist at that time. The word "tiger" was often used in early cheers. The idea of calling for a mighty tiger was a way for yell leaders to bring the animal's powerful strength to the players on the football field. The tiger also built spirit and enthusiasm on the field and in the stands. By 1879 the rallying cry of "tiger" had been used so often in cheers that Princeton adopted the tiger as their symbol or team mascot. Princeton also accepted the growing use of the tiger colors, black and orange, as the school colors.

In 1884 Thomas Peebles, a Princeton graduate, took the locomotive yell along with the sport of football to the University of Minnesota. By the 1890s the University of Minnesota was electing yell captains for each football game. These men called cheers from the sidelines.

In 1898 Jack Campbell, one of the University of Minnesota yell captains, decided that a cheer from the sidelines wouldn't do. Instead, this first-year medical student and frustrated football fan jumped out in front of the crowd during the November 2, 1898, game and led the crowd in a yell. That day modern cheerleading was born.

Campbell used the Minnesota version of the Princeton locomotive yell. University of Minnesota cheerleaders still lead the crowd in this historic cheer. "Rah, Rah, Rah! Sku-u-mah, Hoo-rah! Hoo-rah! Varsity! Varsity! Minn-e-so-tah!"

By the 1900s megaphones became popular with spirit leaders everywhere as a way to increase the sound of the

Lawrence Herkimer performs the "Herkie," a jump he invented, in this 1950s photo. Herkimer, who cheered for Southern Methodist University, went on to found the National Cheerleaders Association in 1948. Today the NCA is part of the National Spirit Group.

voice so that it carried throughout the stands. During this time, the first cheerleader fraternity was organized, an all-male organization called Gamma Sigma.

As football increased in popularity during the first part of the 20th century, so did cheerleading. Yell leaders (still only male) added noisemakers and drums to enliven the roar of the crowd and show football players that their fans were rooting for them to win. In 1914 Lindley Bothwell, a University of Southern California yell leader, directed the first flashcard cheering section. Flashcards prompted the audience with words and slogans that they could shout to encourage the team.

Women finally came on the scene in the 1920s in America and in 1939 in Canada. The University of Minnesota continued to lead innovations as their cheerleaders incorporated tumbling and gymnastics into their cheers.

In the 1930s high school and college cheerleaders discovered paper pom pons, brightly colored strips of crepe paper in the school's colors that were bound together and waved at the crowd. The poms made the arm movements stand out so that fans even in the highest and farthest seats from the field could see the cheerleaders and add their voices to the shout.

Paper pom pons didn't hold up in rainy weather. In the 1960s Fred Gastoff invented the vinyl pom pon, which was introduced by the International Cheerleading Foundation, one of the early cheerleading organizations, that today has become the World Cheerleading Association. Pom pon routines became an important attraction to get the crowd involved. The pom pon, now made out of vinyl or plastic, remains the cheerleader's most used prop.

Lawrence "Herkie" Herkimer, a star cheerleader for Southern Methodist University and a graduate of the school, started the first cheerleaders' organization, the National Cheerleaders Association (NCA), in 1948 in Dallas, Texas. Herkimer had been conducting cheerleading clinics on weekends while teaching gymnastics at SMU. However, the demand for his cheerleading clinics grew so fast that he decided to go into the cheerleading business full-time.

In 1949 Herkimer organized the first cheerleading camp at Sam Houston State University in Huntsville, Texas. Fifty-two girls came to that camp. A speech professor presented tips on speaking in front of an audience, and an English teacher helped them form cheering rhymes. What impressed those 52 girls, however, was Lawrence Herkimer. He combined gymnastics with vigorous motions to demonstrate how to stimulate and direct crowd response. He also showed them a jump that he invented. Today the Herkie jump, where one leg is thrown out forward and the back leg is bent at the knee, is a standard jump that every cheerleader learns.

Once Herkimer trained cheerleaders, they needed a source for sweaters, skirts, and other cheerleading gear. In the early 1950s, Herkimer opened the Cheerleaders Supply Company to offer apparel, equipment, and fundraising items. Today, the Cheerleaders Supply Company, the National Cheerleaders Association, and the dance team division, the National Dance Alliance (NDA), are a multi-million dollar operation that has been combined into the National Spirit Group (NSG). This huge cheerleading conglomerate includes camps, clinics, competitions, equipment, apparel, fundraising materials— every possible item a cheerleader or dance/drill team might need.

From that first camp in Huntsville, Texas, the demand has grown. Today NSG offers 1,500 camps worldwide to guide aspiring and experienced cheerleaders and dance teams. More than any other individual or group, Lawrence "Herkie" Herkimer created the spirit industry. The *New*

For safety and neatness, cheerleaders should wear their hair neatly pulled back so it will not be in the way while performing, and they should never wear jewelry while competing.

York Times called him "a legend in the cheerleading world," and that title still fits.

Herkimer's philosophy was, "I think I can, I think I can," which began when he overcame a stuttering problem. As a student at North Dallas High School, he tried out for high school cheerleader after many hours of hard work and practice in speech class. Although speaking was often a torturous process, he had natural gymnastic ability. Every day on his walk to school along the railroad tracks, he practiced balance by walking on the rails. Soon he developed not only balance but muscle control. His natural gymnastic ability, the confidence he gained working with a speech teacher, and his school popularity helped him gain a squad position the first time he tried out. When Herkie cheered, he never stuttered.

Many years later Herkimer remarked that he never would have believed that one day he would make his

THE HAZARDS OF LONG HAIR AND JEWELRY

As long as women have been cheerleading, they have been asked not to wear jewelry and to keep their hair secured and away from their faces.

Jewelry is distracting, but more important, jewelry can be dangerous, even hazardous to that famous cheerleader smile. Long chains with trinkets attached can fly into a cheerleader's face and chip her teeth. Rings can bruise or injure hands since cheerleaders must clap often. Bracelets and watches can catch in the uniform, snagging it, or worse, trapping an arm that needs to be flung in another direction.

Hair should be kept off the face and secured. A cheerleader can't be messing with her hair, pushing it out of her eyes or face when she's supposed to be leaping into the air, spinning, or flipping over and over in a cartwheel. While performing stunts, the base cheerleader could find herself in a painful predicament if the stunting cheerleader slides down the base's hair on the way to the ground.

living traveling the country lecturing on cheerleading, because he could barely speak clearly when he first began. He followed his "I think I can" philosophy and built an empire. Today he is recognized as the father of modern cheerleading not only for establishing the first camp and supply company for cheerleaders, but for his many innovations.

Some of Herkimer's new ideas were fundraising products to help cheerleaders pay for their uniforms, pom pons, and summer camp fees. When Herkimer created the booster ribbon, he developed a product that cheerleaders could sell and use to boost spirit at the same time. Each week during the days before the Friday night football game, students bought and wore booster ribbons that came in their school colors and bore encouraging slogans such as "Beat the Bears." By the night of the game, the crowd showed up covered in booster ribbons, and the cheerleaders had earned some money.

Herkimer didn't stop with booster ribbons. Soon Cheerleaders Supply Company was offering other fundraising items: megaphones, mascot-printed miniature footballs, booster buttons, and souvenir pennants. In 1967 he marketed paper pom pons on sticks. Cheerleaders sold these pom pons along with booster ribbons. When their team scored a touchdown, fans could wave the colorful pom pons enthusiastically from the stands to congratulate the team and show spirit.

To meet the growing demand for cheerleading uniforms and equipment, Herkimer set up a clothing factory, a knitting mill, and a chenille emblem company. Today,

Cheerleading's huge growth in popularity has created a booming business for companies selling cheerleading uniforms, sneakers, and supplies, as well as those companies offering cheer camps, clinics, and competitions.

Cheerleaders Supply Company, now Cheerleader & DanzTeam, remains a leader in the spirit industry.

Lawrence Herkimer also created the spirit stick, one of the most important cheerleading camp traditions. In 1954 during an NCA Cheer Camp, the first spirit stick was

A National Spirit Group summer camper holds up a spirit stick decorated with ribbons.

awarded. That first stick was a simple tree limb that had been cut, then painted in Herkimer's garage. From such humble origins, the spirit stick has become one of the most coveted camp awards.

During that 1954 camp, one team stood out among the others. They weren't the most talented or technically skilled, but they were the backbone of the camp. In the morning this squad was always the first to arrive to class and the last to leave. They cheered on everyone else, even when they lacked the technical skills themselves. What they symbolized was a vibrant, positive energy that boosted the spirit of everyone in the camp.

Herkimer wanted to reward this team because they, above all others, represented the creed he wanted to instill in all NCA participants: attitude was more important than talent. He met with his camp instructors and discussed his dilemma. He didn't want to change the scoring and award process, but he wanted to acknowledge the impact this team had on everyone in the camp. Spontaneously, he pulled a twig off a tree and declared it the official spirit stick. He knew that a team with such an awesome attitude wouldn't care if they were handed a simple stick.

Today thousands of red, white, and blue wooden dowels are manufactured, but these spirit sticks are as valuable as that first painted tree limb out of Herkimer's garage. The squad who wins the spirit stick may not have the best technical skills or talent. However, these young men and women display the kind of winning attitudes that are as important as any cheerleading skill they might learn.

This winning attitude was what those early yell leaders encouraged their football teams to display. It was the mindset that Jack Campbell used when he jumped out in front of the football crowd and led them in a yell. This cheerleading spirit hasn't stopped growing. It's gotten bigger and stronger and taken exciting new paths.

Competitions

In the 1960s cheerleaders waved pom pons, led chants and cheers using mostly arm motions and jumps, turned the occasional cartwheel, and mounted pyramids. The bulky sweater and pleated skirt were giving way to uniforms that allowed cheerleaders more flexibility. Cartwheels and pyramids were the most difficult skills involved. Cheerleading didn't include gymnastics, complicated stunts, or running tumbling.

Cheerleaders began supporting more teams than just football and basketball. Because they were rooting for other sports as well, high schools needed more squads. The top squad always has been the varsity, usually made

The Ohio State squad competes at UCA Nationals. The UCA sponsored its first National Championships in 1980. Today, hundreds of cheerleading squads participate in the UCA College, High School, and All-Star Nationals each year.

A squad performs at the 2002 NCA College Championships. Cheerleading is more athletic today than ever before as squads incorporate demanding choreography and more complicated moves.

up of juniors and seniors. Some high schools, particularly ones with a big student population, have a varsity squad for each sports team.

The junior varsity or JV squad mostly consists of freshmen and sophomores, and maybe a few juniors. JV squads support JV sports, but sometimes they cheer at the big varsity games, too. Some schools have a freshman squad besides the JV. The freshman squad provides the opportunity for less experienced cheerleaders to perfect their skills. Many schools also have a pep squad, which may include the band and drill team. These students support the cheerleaders to keep spirit lively during games. Often the pep squad is the flashcard section.

By the 1970s, change was rolling like a tumbleweed across America, and it didn't bypass cheerleading. In 1972 Congress passed Title IX, legislation that forbids sex discrimination in schools that receive federal money. Suddenly girls could compete in formerly all-male sports, although in the 1970s not many girls rushed to try out for the football team.

Title IX didn't directly affect cheerleading, since cheerleading was not considered a sport, and males always have cheered right along with females. In fact, Title IX was designed to allow those cheerleaders to move from cheering on the sidelines to playing on the football field, if they chose to try out and had the skills to make the team. The Office of Civil Rights that deals with Title IX athletic issues took the position that cheerleading is not part of the Title IX legislation. Regardless of the government's position, cheerleading's place in Title IX legislation has remained an issue since cheerleading has become more athletic.

Before Title IX cheerleaders could not have been considered athletes. However, in 1974 cheerleading took a new direction led by Jeffrey Webb, a former University of Oklahoma cheerleader. After graduation, Webb worked for the National Cheerleaders Association (NCA) as a

Cheerleading camps help squad members learn new skills that will improve their routines.

general manager for two years. At that time, the NCA was one of the few cheerleading associations. Not long after Lawrence Herkimer established the NCA, Bill Horan formed the American Cheerleaders Association (ACA). The United Spirit Association (USA) opened in 1951, conducting summer camps in the western United States. In 1964 the International Cheerleading Foundation began, and today it is known as the World Cheerleading Association (WCA).

Although these organizations were offering camps and clinics, NCA held the best camps, and Cheerleaders Supply Company remained the top source for uniforms and other gear. Even though Webb worked for NCA, he imagined a more athletic kind of cheerleading. But his vision was not one that NCA supported. Webb, 23, just two years out of college, with not much money, decided to create his own cheerleading company, the Universal Cheerleaders Association (UCA).

"I wanted to modernize cheerleading," Webb said. He wanted to make cheerleading more athletic, entertaining, and "just more exciting to watch."

Webb raised money from family and friends. He set up offices in Memphis, Tennessee, in an area where he already had contacts with schools. That summer, using college and university dormitories, he gathered 4,000 participants who attended 39 UCA camps. Russell High School from Greenup County, Kentucky, was one of the squads attending these first UCA camps. The assistant coach was 24-year old Candy Berry, a graduate of Russell High and a former cheerleader.

WHY IS SUMMER CAMP SO IMPORTANT?

Summer camp always has been a vital training ground for cheerleaders. Camp presents challenges, both mental and physical, that help cheerleaders develop leadership skills, discipline, and organization. Camp provides the opportunity for the squad that was elected in the spring to start working together as a team. Squad members build confidence in their cheerleading abilities, and make new friendships while learning new routines and perfecting old ones.

The first one-day clinic Webb ever taught was for Candy Berry's Russell High School squad. Berry said that the clothes Webb and his instructors wore looked like physical education uniforms, and they still had the "NCA" emblems on them. Webb's group brought their new UCA patches with them, but hadn't had time to sew them on their uniforms. Berry whip-stitched the UCA patches on the uniforms as she sat watching her girls learn the routines.

From that first year of operation, UCA has been profitable. The connection between Candy Berry and UCA has been one filled with success. When UCA launched its first national competition in 1980, the Greenup County High School all-girl varsity squad took second place. Their coach was Candy Berry, who brought her squad back to win over the next three years.

Since the 1980s, the Kentucky powerhouse has often dominated UCA and NCA competitions, with the University of Kentucky, Morehead State, and University of Louisville taking home national trophies. Since 1983, Henry Clay High School in Lexington, Kentucky, has won the large varsity NCA title five times.

Webb's vision was right. Cheerleaders loved mixing cheers with athletic jumps and gymnastic stunts. However, they needed updated uniforms to go with the new kinds of routines UCA camps were teaching. In 1979 Webb launched Varsity Spirit Fashions and Supplies. Webb's only big rival was Lawrence Herkimer's Cheerleaders Supply Company. Varsity offered the standard pom pons and megaphones, but their brightly colored uniforms came in a special material that would stretch rather than tear, and the shoes made shoulder stands more comfortable for the bases.

NCA didn't suffer because they now had a strong competitor. Instead, NCA followed Webb's new direction. NCA was soon teaching athletic routines at their summer camps and offering new types of uniforms that made those stunts and flips possible. As Webb was moving cheerleading in a new direction, NCA was not far behind.

Competition was always part of summer camp. In fact, until the mid-1970s, summer camp was the best opportunity cheerleaders had to compete. Some cheerleading squads competed at local and state levels, but these competitions didn't generate much interest except among the squads involved. NCA dipped its toe in the competition waters in the 1970s with small competitions between squads in the South.

Three years earlier, in 1967, the International Cheerleading Foundation (ICF) had announced the "Top Ten College Squads" and begun its "Cheerleader All America" awards. Not long after, college squads started challenging each other for national championships. In 1978 CBS televised the International Cheerleading Foundation (now WCA) National Collegiate Cheerleading Championships. During this time, some colleges began offering cheerleading scholarships.

In 1983 ESPN began televising UCA high school and college national championships on their sports cable network. Interest in competitions grew as the number of cheerleaders attending summer camps increased. Since

Cheerleaders compete at the 2002 NCA High School Nationals. The number of cheerleading competitions has increased dramatically in recent years, and squads now have more opportunities than ever to test their skills.

the 1950s, many of the summer camp coaches had been college cheerleaders; now many of them were national champions seen on television. As national television got more actively involved, competitions exploded.

NCA began sponsoring national competitions in 1982. The Chick-fil-A Cheer and Dance Collegiate Championship in Daytona Beach, Florida, has become one of its leading events. In 2002 over 180 college cheer and dance teams battled for titles in 11 divisions. These 180 squads were from the United States, Mexico, Japan, and Canada. Since 1997, the finals have been televised on CBS Sports.

The 1980s were a time when spirit squads were not the only groups competing against each other. New cheerleading companies were opening their doors. In 1983

AmeriCheer entered the cheer and dance team industry. Elizabeth Rossetti, who had cheered for Ohio State University, started the company out of her apartment in Columbus, Ohio.

Another Ohio State University cheerleader, Steven Wedge, opened Cheerleaders of America in 1987. Like NCA, UCA, and AmeriCheer, Cheerleaders of America (COA) offered summer camps and clinics as well as regional and national competitions.

Since 1985, the World Cheerleading Association has conducted camps and competitions in the United States, Germany, England, Ireland, and Scotland, and over 4,000 squads have rivaled each other at WCA Nationals at the Opryland Hotel in Nashville, Tennessee.

WCA is one of the few major cheer companies that does not hold its national championships in Florida. From January through the spring, cheerleaders battle for national titles under Florida's sunny skies. UCA meets at Disney World facilities in Orlando, drawing winning high school and college squads like Greenup County and the University of Kentucky. Annually on Easter weekend, Cheerleaders of America (COA) bring mostly high school and youth leagues to the Gaylord Palms Resort, right outside the gates to Disney World. Every March, the AmeriCheer National Cheerleading and Dance Championships occur in the Wide World of Sports Complex at Disney World.

By the close of the 1980s regional and national competitions for junior high and high school squads were firmly established. In 1989 NCA had 4,700 cheerleaders competing for a national prize in Dallas, NCA's hometown. These contestants, who participated in eight divisions, came from 400 high schools and junior highs in 30 states. Most teams had 10 members, but some had as many as 18. No matter the size, they could dance, build pyramids, and tumble while enthusiastically shouting cheers—all within a two minute 15 second time limit.

Jeffrey Webb's vision of a more athletic cheerleader had come to pass. These championship squads completed complex tumbling passes, back tucks, standing back tucks, full flip twists, and any number of mounts.

A standing back tuck is a basic skill on the Greenup County High School all-girl varsity squad. The Greenup squads have become one of the main attractions at UCA nationals. Teams from all over the country come to Florida to compete and to watch the Greenup County girls perform. Coaches want to see what new flip, new tumbling run, or more complex stunt Candy Berry has taught her squad so they can go home and train their squads to do the same routine.

To win a competition on any level requires commitment, skills, and teamwork. The squad must agree to long hours of practice, personal conditioning, and strengthening. Squad members often endure physical pain that results from pushing their young bodies to flip, tumble, and fly high. The excitement, the pride of completing a difficult stunt or routine, and the willingness to forego individual differences, put aside personal problems, and work together as a team make the injuries and other problems surmountable.

Greenup County squads are champions, but they suffer the same injuries and problems as other high school cheerleaders. Regardless of the injuries, the departure of a squad member, or any other problem that may arise, every year Candy Berry pushes her Greenup squads to perform seemingly impossible routines at a championship level. Many times those squads bring home a national trophy; but win or lose, each girl has pushed herself to achieve her best and to overcome doubts and fears.

Cheerleaders can find many opportunities to test their skills. Competitions are not limited to the ones sponsored by the various cheerleading associations that have sprung up since Webb established UCA. College cheerleaders host contests on their campuses for area high school and junior high squads. Many states support cheerleading competitions. Often these contests operate like state basketball or football tournaments.

Still, the biggest and most promoted competitions are those held by professional cheerleading companies like NCA, UCA, and COA. To compete in the national championships, squads must qualify at summer camp or at the regional competitions. Any squad can go to a regional tournament, but they have to qualify to get a national bid. Sometimes squads who are too far away from the regional competition can send a videotape that will certify them for an opportunity to compete at the nationals.

Most associations place their contestants in similar competition divisions. Teams usually range from 5 to 20 members. In the junior high and middle school categories, teams may compete as small or large squads, and as non-mount squads. High schools are divided into freshman, junior varsity, which includes mount and non-mount, and varsity mount and non-mount. Varsity mount squads are usually split into small, medium, and large, and these are usually all-girl squads. Co-ed squads are designated either large or small. A squad that competes in the non-mount category cannot do partner stunts or pyramids.

Many private associations offer competitions for youth and recreation leagues. Most of these youth and recreation divisions begin with sixth grade. Cheerleaders of America (COA) School and Recreation Cheer Teams start the youth division in the fifth grade. COA has also

HOW MUCH HAS THE UCA CHANGED CHEERLEADING ROUTINES?

- The UCA introduced basket tosses, in which three or four bases toss the flyer into the air.

- The UCA invented the elevator, in which two bases hold the feet of one flyer and another base supports her ankles. The bases extend their arms and the flyer stands an arm's length above their heads.

- The UCA invented the liberty, in which the flyer is at arm's length above the heads of three bases. The flyer balances on one leg and bends the other at a 90-degree angle.

- The UCA brought flipping to cheerleading stunts.

- UCA staffers performed the first walk-in liberty heel stretch in national competition.

At the 2000 Americheer Nationals, a squad lifts its flyers in the liberty, a move invented by the Universal Cheerleading Association.

started a Pee Wee division for third and fourth graders, a Junior Pee Wee for second grade and under, and a Mini Pee Wee for kindergarten and under.

In Canada, cheerleading and competition between squads have increased since 1983. The Ontario Cheerleading Federation began in 1986 as school competitive cheerleading was growing throughout the provinces. The Ontario Cheerleading Federation sponsors Regional and Provincial Competitions that offer separate divisions for school and club teams.

Ontario has the greatest number of cheer teams, in part because it also has the largest population in the country.

However, Alberta, British Columbia, New Brunswick, Nova Scotia, Quebec, Manitoba, and Saskatchewan also have active groups.

Since 1983 cheerleading has been recognized as a sport in Alberta. Competitions usually involve high school and junior high cheer teams. A handful of elementary schools have cheer teams, but they do not compete. The junior high has small and large team competition on the A and AA levels. The A level means simple stunts that involve nothing above shoulder level, and no tumbling or tossing. The senior high has small, large, and co-ed divisions. Competitions begin with local schools facing off in City Championships. Winners move on to Provincial Championships.

Competitions are sponsored by the Alberta Cheerleading Association and other provincial associations rather than by cheerleading companies. However, many Canadian cheer teams travel to the United States to attend summer camps and compete.

Canada also has its own cheerleading company, Power Cheerleading Athletics (PCA). Owner David-Lee Tracey grew up with cheerleading competitions. In the 1980s he was a University of Western Ontario (UWO) cheerleader. In 1985 he became the coach of the UWO cheerleaders and founded Power Cheerleading Athletics.

Tracey's University of Western Ontario Cheerleaders from London, Ontario have been Canadian University National Champions for the last 17 years. In 2001 and 2002 they won the NCA Nationals International Division. Every summer, Tracey and his UWO cheerleaders go to the NCA camp at the University of Louisville in Kentucky.

Since 1986 PCA has sponsored the National Collegiate Cheerleading Championships. Teams from universities throughout Canada compete for national titles. Ninety-five percent of the collegiate cheer programs attend this national competition, which moves to a different university every two years.

In 2002, PCA held the first Canadian national high school championships. PCA also holds summer camps at sites in Ontario, Alberta, Nova Scotia, Quebec, and British Columbia.

Spirit squads now have many opportunities to challenge each other. In 2002, about 30 percent of U.S. high school squads participated in national competitions.

Since Title IX changed the face of athletics, female cheerleaders have been working hard to elevate cheerleading to sports status. Competitions have been an avenue for this to occur. However, for some of these talented young women and men, school competitions, no matter how difficult the level, are not enough.

All-Star Cheerleading

A new breed of cheerleader has stepped out of the sidelines and seized center field. In the late 1980s all-star cheerleading started, and like that siss-boom-bah skyrocket yell of long, long ago, all-star teams have shot higher in the air than the lightest-weight flyer ever could. When the all-stars entered the scene, the number of competitions exploded, and they haven't settled down yet.

All-star squads are not affiliated with any sports team or school system, and their season lasts year round. All-stars are usually divided into three groups: youth for ages under 12, juniors ages 12 to 14, and seniors ages 15 to 17. These talented young people cheer for one

Many of the top cheerleading squads aren't affiliated with a school at all—instead, they are all-star teams sponsored by gyms, clubs, and other businesses.

reason only—to win cheerleading competitions. Teams can be as few as five and as many as 35 young men and women, all with one goal in mind: winning.

All-stars began unofficially in 1986 at NCA Nationals. Some teams showed up to compete at NCA Nationals that year who were not part of a high school's squad. These teams were made up of high school girls who had started out years earlier in youth Pop Warner cheerleading. Their coaches were NCA instructors who trained their teams in gyms where they worked part-time. The coaches wanted to give their teams the opportunity to compete.

In 1986 there were no categories for non-school teams. However, that year NCA allowed these non-school groups to compete in the high school division. One of the teams came in third. Not long after, NCA created an

SKILLS FOR ALL-STAR NOVICES

Cheerleaders of America (COA) limits Novice All Star Cheer Teams to standing tumbling that involves back handsprings, back handspring series, jumps into back handsprings, and back handsprings into jumps, but doesn't allow beginners to do tucks of any kind, including back handspring back tucks. COA will let beginners do basket tosses as long as it's a basic single toe touch, ball outs, and pencils, but no scissor kicks or twists of any kind. COA limits beginners to stunts involving single twist cradles from extensions or doubled-footed cupies, but won't let them do any double twist cradles of any kind and no single twist cradles from one-legged stunts of any kind.

all-star division for juniors, seniors, and co-ed as more of these talented non-school affiliated teams wanted the opportunity to compete. NCA was the first company to start the all-star program. By the late 1980s, NCA began their first annual All-Star National Championships.

In 2002 Cheerleaders of America president Steven Wedge estimated that all-stars accounted for 70 percent of COA national competition.

"Today some 2,500 gyms or clubs nationwide have cheering squads," says Bill Seely of Varsity Spirit Corporation, the parent company of the UCA.

Many of these gyms exist for no other reason than to train all-star teams, and they don't take just anybody who shows up. Hopeful all-stars must audition for a spot on the team. Coaches are looking for males and females who can perform a high-powered blend of gymnastics, dance, and athletics. These private gyms are found in major cities throughout the United States and in several Canadian provinces. Many parents willingly drive an hour or more to bring their sons and daughters to practice. They also pay gym fees and raise funds to cover the expenses of competition.

The nation's largest competitive-cheer gym is Cheer Athletics in Dallas, Texas. Dallas is Lawrence Herkimer's home town and the heart of cheerleading country. Herkimer didn't start the all-star movement, but the National Cheerleaders Association (NCA) still holds its biggest contest—the NCA All-Star Cheerleading Championship, televised on the USA cable network. The UCA, AmeriCheer, Cheerleaders of America (COA), and the World Cheerleading Association (WCA) are among the major cheerleading associations sponsoring all-star competitions. In Canada, all-stars are popular and growing, with Power Cheerleading Athletics (PCA) sponsoring regional and national contests.

Although Cheer Athletics trains all-star teams who consistently win national championships, it operates like most all-star gyms. Kids from ages 3 to 18 try out for one of Cheer Athletics' dozen teams, which are divided by age and skill. These teams compete in regional meets in the fall to qualify for national competitions in the spring. Judges rate teams on a combination of dance, showmanship, and skills.

Routines set to fast-paced rock and techno music last no longer than two and a half minutes. Muscular bases hold girls who dazzle judges with their heel stretches and scorpion poses. Bases toss a featherweight flyer 20 feet in the air. As the flyer floats high above her team, she's likely to throw a "double full," a back flip combined with two aerial twists.

The girls and guys who make these elite all-star squads are highly skilled dancers, gymnasts, and athletes. They condition and strength-train like star athletes. In fact, some of them are star athletes who once played sports such as football, basketball, and soccer. Some all-stars have dropped out of their school squads or turned down spots on sports teams. Wherever they come from, they all want the athletic challenge of all-star cheerleading.

Many are looking for college scholarships. The all-star team is one of the best avenues to scholarship money, since college recruiters routinely attend all-star championships to scout for cheerleaders. Parents willingly drive the distances and pay the gym fees in the hopes that the regional and national all-star competitions will lead to college scholarships for their children.

Girls need co-ed stunting experience to attract college recruiters, and they don't get it on all-girl varsity high school squads. All-star gyms attract a good number of males for co-ed all-star teams, which provide these female athletes with plenty of co-ed opportunities. The males find all-star cheerleading can be as tough as facing a linebacker on the football field.

THE ALL-STAR OPEN DIVISION

Cheerleaders participating in the open division of an all-star competition cannot compete on any other cheer team, and with good reason. Many of the open teams are made up of college cheerleaders, college and all-star coaches, and any number of champion cheerleaders who have graduated from high school. Open divisions follow college guidelines and are exempt from the National Federation Spirit Safety Rules. That means pyramids can go up three levels. Ages start at 18 and go up from there; participants have to be at least high school graduates age 18 or older.

During the 2002 NCA Chick-fil-A All-Star Cheerleading Championship, the owner of Gymtyme, an all-star gym in Louisville, Kentucky, was the oldest member of the Gymtyme open team. This forty-year-old man held the flyers aloft as agilely as any younger man. He helped his all-star team place second in the open co-ed competition.

Many school systems throughout the country and in Canada have banned the use of gymnastic stunts in cheerleading routines. This move, although understandable given the safety issues involved in some of the stunts, has driven more students to drop the school squad and join the all-star team. This new breed of cheerleaders doesn't want to be hindered by safety or any other restrictions that limit the routines they can perform.

The risks of injury are high. A November 6, 2000, *Time* magazine article stated that "the rate of cheerleading injuries, caused in large part by increasingly elaborate stunts, was six times as high as that of football injuries among high school kids."

A May 21, 2001 *Newsweek* magazine article supports *Time*'s claim. It describes a 17-year-old Cheer Athletics flyer who suffered "a dislocated hip, fractured kneecap, and two ruptured discs." In the article Jody Melton, president of Cheer Athletics, says, "Coaches and rulemakers are boosting safety precautions as the sport matures."

All-stars have as many or more injuries than traditional cheerleaders, but they don't have to worry about chanting yells because calling out cheers usually isn't a competition element. In fact, NCA doesn't require all-star teams to call a cheer. *American Cheerleader* magazine senior editor Alyssa Roeniak said, "It's not really what they're about anyway. So in many cases, they'd prefer to compete just to music."

All-star cheerleading has also drawn adults to the private gyms because they want to coach top-notch athletes. Some of the all-star coaches left their schools

A male Flyers cheerleader holds a female squad member overhead during a co-ed competition at the 2000 AmeriCheer Nationals. In the United States, all-star cheerleading is the fastest growing segment of the cheerleading industry.

All-star cheerleaders are highly skilled athletes who train year round for competitions. Unlike other cheerleaders, they don't actually call out any chants or cheers. Instead, they focus on gymnastics, tumbling, and stunting.

because they were tired of the many rules and teaching obligations.

One of the reasons all-star cheerleading has grown so dramatically is the designation of cheerleading as a sport. The downside of making cheerleading a sport is that high school squads have been hurt. The additional funding was a plus; however, cheerleaders now are bound by the same rules and regulations as sports teams. For instance, in the Maryland counties that have named cheerleading a sport, cheerleaders can't attend competitions farther than 300 miles away from their school. They can practice only between given dates and for designated amounts of time. Since cheerleading really doesn't have a season, many squads have to try out once in the fall and again in the spring in order to meet eligibility rules.

In Canada, provinces that designate cheerleading as a sport do not allow cheerleaders to be on the school squad and on an all-star team. In Alberta, the Alberta Schools Athletic Association rules that athletes cannot participate on a club team, in this case the all-star team, and play the same sport in school during the same season. Cheerleading season doesn't end in the fall; it's a year-round sport, so technically, cheerleaders can't be on an all-star team, too. Alberta doesn't have the distance restriction; in fact, many Alberta high schools have traveled across the border to compete in UCA or NCA national competitions and attend summer camps.

In the United States, all-star cheerleading is the fastest growing segment of the cheerleading industry today. Jeffrey Webb's vision of a more athletic cheerleader has surpassed even what he imagined. UCA, NCA, and the other private associations continue to find ways to make cheerleading more exciting, and all-stars will probably lead the way.

Cheerleading Today

Cheerleaders in the 21st century don't stand on the sidelines; they perform on center stage. They are dancers, stunters, gymnasts, cross trainers, choreographers, writers, artists, and organizers. Some are bases strong enough to lift people their own weight—sometimes above their heads or in one hand. Others are so light they can be tossed twenty feet into the air, flip, and neatly turn a double twist as they fall into the bases' arms.

Some become all-stars, while others continue the time-honored tradition of rooting for the home team. They still share with spirit leaders who've gone before them the ability to whip up the crowd's spirits with their bright

As cheerleading becomes more and more athletic, safety guidelines have been developed to minimize the risk of injury. Most cheerleaders follow the safety guidelines created by the American Association of Cheerleading Coaches and Advisors (AACCA).

53

smiles and winning attitudes. Cheerleaders always will need to build that special link with the crowd, whether they are elite all-stars dazzling their spectators with incredible stunts and tumbles, or high school squads pumping up the Friday night football crowd.

In 2002, 95 percent of all cheerleaders were female, and 5 percent were male. A few years earlier only 2 percent of all cheerleaders were male. By 2002 about 50 cheerleading companies offered these male and female cheerleaders every variety of uniform and cheer

MUSIC CITY LIGHTNING WHEELCHEERLEADERS

They're pretty. They wear sweaters with short pleated skirts and cheer shoes. They wave pom pons while they cheer and dance. Twice a month they practice their hello cheer and halftime dance. They act like every other cheerleader encouraging her team to victory, except these nine girls, ages 5 to 16, perform their routines from wheelchairs. Decorated with a silver lightning bolt on black wheel covers, their wheelchairs even show spirit.

The Music City Lightning Wheelcheerleaders of Lebanon, Tennessee, are the first wheelchair cheerleading and dance troupe. Formed in 2001, they support the Music City Thunder Wheelchair Basketball Team. The Easter Seals of Middle Tennessee sponsor this lively group. Coached by Bethany Hoppe, the Wheelcheerleaders are part of a state-based program, Athletes Building Life Experiences (ABLE).

Everywhere they perform, the fans love them. A group of young girls came up and asked for autographs after they cheered at Vanderbilt University for a halftime show.

gear, any number of summer camps, and a variety of competition opportunities. Jeffrey Webb's Universal Cheerleaders Association (UCA) is the biggest, but the National Cheerleaders Association (NCA), and Cheerleaders of America (COA) are not far behind. Half a million of these cheerleaders attend summer camps sponsored by these private associations.

In the early 1990s six Canadian cheerleading companies existed: Cheer Ltd. (Canadian division), Cheerleading Dynamics, Cheer Energy, Canadian Cheerleading Assembly, and Top Level Cheerleading. By 2002, only David-Lee Tracey's Power Cheerleading Athletics has survived. Part of the reason is that Canada is so spread out geographically. Fifty-four percent of the country's population lives in Ontario, and that's where the heart of cheerleading resides. Many of the other provinces have schools that support cheerleading programs, especially in British Columbia, Alberta, Quebec, and Nova Scotia. But they are tiny compared to the number in Ontario.

All-star programs continue to increase. In 2002 about 1,500 all-star programs operated inside 613 gyms somewhere in the United States. In Canada, Power Cheerleading Athletics operates the only all-star cheer gym. Owner David-Lee Tracey coaches the Power Cheer Gym junior and senior All-Star Vipers.

In 2002 only about 20 all-star programs existed in Canada. All-star teams have not skyrocketed in Canada like they have in the United States. Many Canadian high school cheer teams provide the athletic and gymnastic opportunities cheerleaders want, so all-stars is not as attractive an option. In some of the other provinces, young men and women often join all-stars because their schools don't have cheer teams. Canadian all-star programs, though small in number, are growing as some Canadian cheerleaders are choosing the elite training opportunities all-star teams provide. No Canadian or American school program can offer cheerleaders the competitive edge of all-star contests.

In 1972 Title IX legislation offered girls the chance to play guys' sports. What happened? There still aren't many girls in football helmets, but about three million girls and guys are wearing cheerleader uniforms in the United States, and a growing number in Canada and other nations.

By 2002 competitions numbered 72 national or regional contests for college, high school, junior high, and youth teams, up from eight in 1988. But as the competition opportunities have increased, so has the number of injuries.

In 1988, the American Association of Cheerleading Coaches and Advisors (AACCA) was founded. This non-profit educational association's members are representatives from the leading cheerleading companies and the over 50,000 cheerleading coaches who direct youth, junior high, high school, and college cheerleading programs. The UCA helped the AACCA to publish the first comprehensive cheerleading safety manual. Today, most of the spirit industry and its participants follow these safety guidelines. The AACCA continues to guide coaches and school administrators in maintaining safe and highly effective programs that try to please all those involved.

The National Federation of State High School Associations assists high school and middle school dance and cheer coaches in managing risk, promoting good sportsmanship and citizenship, and providing professional development. Both the AACCA and the NFHS publish safety rules and guidelines to keep cheerleading, dance, and drill teams safe.

Steven Wedge, President of Cheerleaders of America, believes that knowledgeable, educated coaches are a cheerleader's best defense against injury. Cheerleading is no more dangerous than any other physical activity as long as the adult directing it has been properly trained.

Cheerleaders are dedicated individuals who bring intelligence along with athletic and gymnastic skills to their high school squads or all-star teams. Many high school and all-star cheerleaders are chosen by their school faculties to be members of the National Honor Society. These National Honor Society members have high B or above averages, participate in school and community activities, and show character qualities that count—dependability, honesty, and courtesy.

The AACCA surveys show that cheerleaders are campus leaders who participate in other student activities and often play another sport. Consistently, their grades are higher, and more high school cheerleaders go on to college than the general population of students.

Since February 1995, when *American Cheerleader* published its first edition, there has been plenty written

Though cheerleading has changed dramatically over time, it is still about showing spirit, whether it's for your school, your gym, or your own squad.

about cheerleading. Today this bi-monthly magazine has over a million readers. *American Cheerleader* has contributed to the growth of the spirit industry and become an excellent resource for spirit leaders and their coaches. In the spring of 2001, Lifestyle Ventures, the publisher of *American Cheerleader,* launched *Junior Cheerleader,* a quarterly magazine for ages 8 to 12 who want to know all about the fun of cheerleading.

The debate about whether cheerleading is a sport or not continues. Many states want to leave cheerleading as a school activity. For school squads that want to compete nationally, this is positive. In states where cheerleading is a sport, school squads can't attend national competitions unless they are less than 300 miles away. At this time, allowing cheerleading to float between an activity and a sport is the best of both worlds. Cheerleaders perform routines that are definitely athletic, but they aren't required to follow the strict rules that govern most sports. Instead, they follow their own rules.

Many Canadian coaches agree with their American counterparts. Alberta and Nova Scotia wrestle with restricted training rules since cheerleaders can't train out of season. But when does a cheerleader's season end? It doesn't, and that's one of the issues. What has happened is that many talented Canadian cheerleaders leave the school squad and join all-star teams. The debate goes on in Canada and the United States, and it's not likely to end soon—if ever.

Whether all-star or a member of the varsity squad, cheerleaders are graceful, strong athletes and gymnasts with plenty of bounce, energy, and coordination. These yell leaders are no longer all male, but they still can bring a crowd to their feet. They tumble, flip, and fly. Some of today's best gymnasts aren't springing across a mat or perching dangerously on a balance beam. Instead, they are wearing a cheerleader uniform.

Glossary

base – A person who has contact with the floor and supports another person.

basket toss – Toss of a flyer into the air involving three to four tossers, two of whom have their hands interlocked.

choreography – The planning of the steps of a dance routine.

criteria – Rules by which something can be judged.

flyer – A person who is elevated into the air by the base to perform a mount.

handspring – A somersault in which only a hand or the hands touch the ground.

heel stretch – A stunt performed by the flyer, who grabs the arch of her foot and extends her leg while being supported by the bases.

mount – Any skill in which one or more persons (the bases) support one or more top persons (flyers).

partner stunt – A mount that involves only two people.

pyramid – A stunt involving more than one mount.

standing back tuck – A tumbling position where the body is bent at the hips and the knees are held tightly to the chest.

stunting – Any maneuver or set of maneuvers including tumbling, mounting, a pyramid, or a toss.

synchronized – Moving or happening at the same time or speed.

tumbling – Moves involving forward or backward rolls, flips, handstands, standing back tucks, or tucks.

Internet Resources

http://www.albertacheerleading.ca
The Web site of the Alberta Cheerleading Association (ACA).

http://cheerleading.about.com/index.htm
An About.com directory of hundreds of cheerleading Web sites.

http://www.americancheerleader.com
The official Web site of *American Cheerleader* magazine features message boards, chat, and a wide variety of articles available to subscribers.

http://www.cheerhome.com
CheerHome.com features news, message boards, articles, and information on cheerleading camps, competitions, and college programs.

http://www.cheerleading.net
Cheerleading.net offers links to hundreds of Web sites for cheerleaders and coaches at all levels.

http://www.nationalspirit.com
The National Spirit Group is the parent company of the National Cheerleaders Association, the group begun in 1948 by Lawrence Herkimer.

http://www.ocf.on.ca
The Web site of the Ontario Cheerleading Federation (OCF).

http://www.uca.com
The Universal Cheerleaders Association is a leader in cheerleading safety and stunt innovation and one of the largest cheerleading camp providers and competition sponsors in the world.

http://www.varsity.com
Resources for both cheerleading and dance provided by Varsity Spirit, a leading supplier of uniforms.

Further Reading

French, Stephanie Breaux. *The Cheerleading Book.* Chicago: Contemporary Books, 1995.

McElroy, James T. *We've Got Spirit: The Life and Times of America's Greatest Cheerleading Team.* New York: Berkley Books, 1999.

Neil, Randy, and Elaine Hart. *The Official Cheerleader's Handbook.* New York: Simon & Schuster, 1986.

Rusconi, Ellen. *Cheerleading.* New York: Children's Press, 2001.

Scott, Kieran. *Ultimate Cheerleading.* New York: Scholastic, Inc., 1998.

Index

DORIS VALLIANT teaches English at Easton High School in Easton, Maryland. She writes books for young people and articles for regional publications. She wasn't a cheerleader in high school, but two of her best friends were. She shouted with them at the Friday night football games and performed a skit or two at pep rallies.